KANGAROO TO THE RESCUE!

And More True Stories of Amazing Animal Heroes

Moira Rose Donohue

NATIONAL GEOGRAPHIC

WASHINGTON, D.C.

Published by the
National Geographic Society

Gary E. Knell, *President and
Chief Executive Officer*
John M. Fahey, *Chairman of the Board*
Declan Moore, *Executive Vice President;
President, Publishing and Travel*
Melina Gerosa Bellows, *Publisher and Chief
Creative Officer, Books, Kids, and Family*

Prepared by the Book Division
Hector Sierra, *Senior Vice President and
General Manager*
Nancy Laties Feresten, *Senior Vice President,
Kids Publishing and Media*
Eva Absher-Schantz, *Design Director,
Kids Publishing and Media*
Jay Sumner, *Director of Photography,
Kids Publishing and Media*
Jennifer Emmett, *Vice President,
Editorial Director, Kids Books*
R. Gary Colbert, *Production Director*
Jennifer A. Thornton, *Director of Managing
Editorial*

Staff for This Book
Shelby Alinsky, *Project Editor*
Marfé Ferguson Delano, *Editor*
Jay Sumner, *Photo Editor*
Callie Broaddus, *Associate Designer*
Ruth Ann Thompson, *Designer*
Paige Towler, *Editorial Assistant*
Erica Holsclaw, *Special Project Assistant*
Sanjida Rashid, *Design Production Assistant*
Margaret Leist, *Photo Assistant*
Grace Hill, *Associate Managing Editor*
Joan Gossett, *Production Editor*
Lewis R. Bassford, *Production Manager*
Susan Borke, *Legal and Business Affairs*

Production Services
Phillip L. Schlosser, *Senior Vice President*
Chris Brown, *Vice President,
NG Book Manufacturing*
George Bounelis, *Senior Production Manager*
Nicole Elliott, *Director of Production*
Rachel Faulise, *Manager*
Robert L. Barr, *Manager*

For more information, please visit
nationalgeographic.com, call
1-800-NGS LINE (647-5463), or write
to the following address:

National Geographic Society
1145 17th Street N.W.
Washington, D.C. 20036-4688 U.S.A.

Visit us online at
nationalgeographic.com/books

For librarians and teachers:
ngchildrensbooks.org

**National Geographic supports K–12
educators with ELA Common Core
Resources. Visit natgeoed.org/
commoncore for more information.**

More for kids from National Geographic:
kids.nationalgeographic.com

For information about special discounts for
bulk purchases, please contact National
Geographic Books Special Sales:
ngspecsales@ngs.org

For rights or permissions inquiries, please
contact National Geographic Books Subsidiary
Rights: ngbookrights@ngs.org

Trade paperback
ISBN: 978-1-4263-1913-6
Reinforced library edition
ISBN: 978-1-4263-1915-0

Printed in China
14/RRDS/1

LULU: KANGAROO to the Rescue

Lulu takes a break from hopping to stretch out in the sun.

Lulu is happy to hang out with Luke Richards and his parents.

Chapter 1

Luke Richards and his friends were driving home late one evening.

"Watch out!" one of the boys yelled. "There's something in the road!"

Squee!! The driver hit the brakes and swerved. He avoided hitting the lump in the road.

"Pull over, mate," Luke said. He wanted to move whatever was in the road out of the way. Luke hopped out of the car.

The lump turned out to be a dead kangaroo. That would be a shock if you lived in the United States. But Luke lived in Australia. Millions of kangaroos live there, too. Unfortunately, sometimes they wander into the road in front of cars and trucks.

Luke was sad to see the kangaroo, but he knew he had to move it out of the way. He grabbed the animal by the tail and dragged it to the side of the road. It was heavy. Full-grown eastern gray kangaroos, or "roos," as they say in Australia, weigh about 145 pounds (66 kg).

Then Luke saw something amazing. The kangaroo's belly twitched. Kangaroos are a kind of mammal known as marsupials (sounds like mar-SOO-pee-ulz). Females have a pouch across their bellies. That's where they keep their babies, called joeys (sounds like JOE-eez). Luke put his hand in the pouch. Gently, he removed a joey. It had survived the accident!

Luke didn't think his parents would be happy if he brought the joey home. But he looked into the animal's frightened eyes. He just couldn't leave the little roo behind.

The joey was about the size of a cat. Luke wrapped it in his sweater. He climbed back into the car.

When he got home, Luke tiptoed into the house. He didn't want to wake his parents. He got some newspapers and covered

Did You Know?

When it's born, a baby kangaroo is hairless. It takes several months before its fur grows in.

the floor of his room. He offered the joey some water. Then he tucked the little roo snugly into his sweater. He draped the sweater over his bedpost. He hoped it would feel like the mother's pouch. Within minutes, both he and the joey were asleep.

The next morning, Luke's mother, Lynn, opened the door to his bedroom. It was a mess. She frowned. "Luke?" she called in a voice that said he was in trouble. Luke sat up. And like bread in a toaster, the joey popped up, too.

"I've got a little friend, mum," said Luke.

"So I see," his mother sputtered.

Luke's family lived on a small farm. It was about 90 miles (145 km) west of the city of Melbourne. The farm was surrounded by land that was covered with wild plants and trees. This is known as "the bush" in Australia. Animals from the bush often wandered onto the farm. Sometimes Luke and his sister, Celeste, would find an injured one.

"They brought home a lot of king parrots that were hurt," said their father, Len. Once Luke and Celeste found a wounded opossum. They even rescued a wombat. They brought them to their father. He showed them how to nurse the animals.

But a baby kangaroo was another story. This joey was a female. She was about three months old. Normally, a joey doesn't even peek out of its pouch until it is four months old. At five or six months, it climbs out into the world. But only for a short time. After a few minutes, the joey dives headfirst back into the pouch. The joey doesn't leave the pouch for good until it's about ten months old.

This joey would need a lot of care. Luke's parents wondered if he would have enough time to take care of her.

"I want to do it," Luke told them. His mother and father discussed it. They were proud of him for wanting to take care of the roo. Len and Lynn decided to give him a chance.

Lynn found an old sleeping bag. She cut it up. She sewed a pouch for the baby kangaroo. Luke slipped the joey in. She seemed to like it. It was more like a mother's pouch than Luke's sweater had been.

Next, Luke tried to feed the joey milk from a bottle. She refused.

Pouch Parents

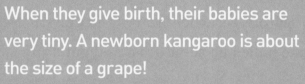

Marsupials are mammals, like dogs and people. Like most mammals, they give birth to live babies. But marsupials are different from other mammals in one big way. Marsupial females have pouches. When they give birth, their babies are very tiny. A newborn kangaroo is about the size of a grape!

Right after birth, a marsupial baby crawls into its mother's pouch. The mother carries her babies in her pouch for months. Most of the marsupials in the world live in Australia. The largest marsupial is the red kangaroo. Koalas and wombats are also marsupials.

Poor baby. She was probably missing her mother's milk. But Luke didn't give up. And after a couple of days, the joey finally drank the milk. Now that she was drinking milk, Luke had to feed her often—even in the middle of the night.

After taking the bottle for a while, the joey suddenly stopped. Maybe she's ready for real food, Luke thought. He knew that kangaroos eat tender leaves and grass. Luke pulled up some grass and put it in his room.

The next morning, Len heard his son call out, "She's eating grass!" The joey was growing up.

Luke continued to take care of the little roo. His family helped. They held her, petted her, and snuggled her. She cuddled with them on the couch. They were growing very attached to her.

But after a few months, the Richards family had another discussion.

"I think it's time we turned the joey out," Len said. He knew she needed to return to the wild.

No one wanted to see her go. She was a family pet now. But they agreed it was the right thing to do. The next morning, Len opened the gate. The family watched silently as the joey hopped through it. She bounded over the next fence. She bounced high over the next one.

She was gone.

But three hours later, something was hopping around the Richardses' yard. The joey was back!

In the Richardses' backyard, Lulu perks up her big ears.

Chapter 2

HOP ALONG

The Richardses were thrilled to have the joey back. But if she was going to stay, they needed to make some changes.

Len said, "She needs a name." They had another family discussion. No one said anything at first.

"What about 'Lulu'?" Lynn asked. Everyone liked the name right away. Then Lynn said, "She needs to move outside."

The joey wasn't housebroken. Lynn was tired of the messes Lulu made in the house. She thought if she hung a cloth pouch on the porch, Lulu could hop in and out during the night. Then Luke wouldn't have to cover his floor with newspapers.

Lulu seemed to like the idea right away. She had a little freedom. But she had her family close by, too.

The joey grew. During the day, she roamed freely around the farm. The Richardses had an apple tree on the farm. King parrots liked to perch in the tree. They munched on the fresh, crunchy apples.

But Lulu wanted the crisp apples, too. She would jump up and scare the birds away. Then she would pull the ripest apples off the tree for herself.

Sometimes Lulu hopped the fences and took off for the bush. But at six in the

Did You Know?

Female kangaroos are called "flyers." The males are called "boomers."

evening, the Richardses would hear a loud banging on the door. Lulu kicked the door with her feet at dinnertime every night. Then she bounded inside the house. Lulu headed to the pantry first. She wanted a snack of her favorite "teddy bear" biscuits (sounds like BIS-kits), or cookies.

She reached for the snack jar with her front paws. Kangaroos are one of very few bipedal (sounds like bye-PED-ul) animals. That means that they walk on two feet, like humans. They use their front paws to hold things. They also use them if they are walking on all fours, called "slow walking."

Big Roos, Little Roos

There are millions of kangaroos in Australia. In fact, more kangaroos live there than people! There are more than 60 kinds, or species (sounds like SPEE-sheez), of kangaroo. They come in many sizes. The two largest kinds are gray kangaroos and red kangaroos (shown above). They can stand as tall as a six-foot (1.8-m) person and usually weigh 120 to 150 pounds (54 to 68 kg). They live in herds called "mobs." The smallest kangaroo is the musky rat kangaroo. It's only about the size of—you guessed it—a rat.

"Lulu, be careful," Len would tell the roo. But a few times he didn't get there fast enough, and Lulu dropped the jar. After she broke a couple of jars, Len got a plastic box for the biscuits.

The Richardses kept a big bowl of fruit for the family. It usually sat on the dinner table. Lulu loved fruit. She stood high on her back legs. She stretched out her front paws to grab the bowl. But if she couldn't reach it, Lulu knew a clever trick.

Slowly she tugged the tablecloth. Bit by bit, the bowl moved closer. Then Lulu picked through the fruit. She especially liked nectarines (sounds like nek-tuh-REENS) and bananas. But she wanted the ripest fruit. If she bit into a piece that wasn't ripe enough, she put it back and took another! Then she held the fruit with her front paws and nibbled around the pit.

The Richardses also had a dog. Bustie was a cocker spaniel (sounds like SPAN-yul). Lulu liked to play with Bustie. She chased him. She batted at him with her front paws. She even grabbed his silky ears. He didn't mind. And sometimes he played with her, too.

Lulu sat with the family and Bustie in the living room every evening. Like most dogs, Bustie liked to lay by the fireplace. Lulu liked it there, too. If Bustie was already curled up in front of the fire, Lulu would nudge him out of the way. After all, she was a lot bigger. Then Lulu would lay down with her front legs under her. As she relaxed, her head went down and her paws went out. Soon she was asleep.

"That's how I knew she really trusted us," said Len.

The Richardses never tried to train Lulu to go to the bathroom outside, like a dog. Somehow, she just figured it out. Whenever she wanted to go outside, she went to the door and stood there. If they didn't notice right away, she knocked on it.

When the family went to bed, they put Lulu outside. She had outgrown her pouch on the porch. But she still slept nearby.

As time passed, Lulu became especially fond of Len, even though Luke had taken care of her when she was a baby. During the day, she followed Len around.

Len went about his chores. Lulu went too.
He checked on the vegetable gardens.
Lulu bounded beside him. When Len
looked in on the farm animals, the
kangaroo hopped along.

Len got used to having Lulu with him. Every morning, before he went to do farm work, he would step outside and whistle for her. Then

he called, "Lulu! Lulu!" Lulu was usually
in the bush, eating grass.

When Lulu heard the whistle, she
would stop whatever she was doing and
listen carefully. Kangaroos have ears that
can turn in every direction. This helps

them hear enemies that might be creeping up, such as the wild dogs called dingoes.

After listening closely for a moment, Lulu would bound toward Len's voice. When she reached him, she batted at him and gave him a smooch. Len would pet and hug her. He might even have a treat for her. Sometimes he had an ice pop for her!

Lulu and Len had a very special bond. In time, Lulu would prove how strong that bond was.

Special friends
Lulu and Len
shake hands,
or paws.

Chapter 3

BIG FOOT

When Lulu was about four years old, a huge storm blew through the Richardses' farm. It poured. And the winds howled.

The next morning, Len and Lulu went out to see how much damage the storm had caused. The two friends looked in on the animals. They were fine. Next they checked the fences. *They might need some work,* Len thought. Finally Len and

Lulu walked around the big gum trees.

Gum trees are also called eucalyptus (sounds like you-kuh-LIP-tuss) trees. They grow very tall. Their leaves are the favorite food of koalas. And they produce an oil that is used to make many medicines. But they don't grow chewing gum!

The wind had blown down a lot of branches. Len would have to come back and pick them up. He noticed a broken branch in one of the gum trees. It seemed to be hanging off the other branches. It was too high and too big for Len to pull down by himself. He poked it, but it didn't move. It was stuck. He decided to work on it later, too. He turned his back on it.

Wham! The branch crashed down— right onto Len. It hit him over the head.

It knocked him to the ground. And it knocked him out. Len was unconscious (sounds like un-CON-shuss).

Somehow Lulu knew that Len was seriously hurt. She hopped into action. Kangaroos don't make a lot of sounds. Sometimes Lulu made a little click-click sound. But that day, Lulu made a great noise. *Cro-ack!!!* She barked. She croaked. She kept making noise for 15 minutes. Finally, Lynn became worried.

"Something's wrong!" Lynn said. She took off in the direction of the sound.

Len's nephew Brendan was visiting. He sprinted as fast as he could and got there first. Lynn and her nephew were amazed by what they found. Lulu was standing by Len's head, barking.

Put Up Your Paws

Sometimes two male kangaroos want the same female kangaroo. Then they will fight each other. The males lean back on their tails. They kick with their big rear feet. And they grab at each other with their front paws. It looks as if they are boxing. They don't usually hurt each other. But sometimes they scratch each other with their sharp claws. The boxing kangaroo is a popular symbol in Australia. It's even been used on some flags!

Len was frothing, or spitting up, at the mouth. If he had rolled onto his back, he probably would have choked. But Lulu had used her big feet to keep Len on his side. And safe. No one knows if Lulu tipped Len onto his side. Perhaps he fell that way. And she just used her big feet to keep him that way. However it happened, Lulu did the right thing.

Lynn called for an ambulance. It came quickly. The nurses could tell that Len had a serious head injury. He needed to see a doctor right away. So they whisked him to the nearest helicopter port. A helicopter flew him to a hospital in Melbourne.

Len pulled through. He recovered completely. But he says that if it hadn't been for Lulu, he would have died that day.

Len and his family couldn't believe what Lulu had done. They told their friends. Soon, local newspaper reporters heard the story. They wrote articles about Lulu. Then reporters came from all over the world: Sweden, the United States, even China! They met Lulu. They took her picture. They even made a video about her.

Sometimes the fuss was too much for Lulu. She would go to the door. She would look at Len to ask him to let her out. Or she would lick her front paws. Len knew that meant she was nervous. Then Len would tell everyone that Lulu needed a break.

People who heard Lulu's story were impressed. There were always stories about heroic dogs. And sometimes other household or farm animals rescued their owners. But kangaroos are wild animals. People don't generally keep roos as pets, even in Australia.

Animal experts were amazed. How was this even possible? A wild animal vet in Australia said he had never heard of it happening. But Lulu was a female kangaroo. A human family had raised her. Experts agreed that the roo must have formed a bond of trust with the family.

The Richardses know that's what happened with Lulu. She had no kangaroo family. And she never wanted to join other kangaroos. One time Len saw a mob of kangaroos nearby. They hopped toward Lulu. She turned and hopped away. Then she went into the house. As Len watched, she loped to the window.

What's she up to? Len wondered. Lulu tugged at the curtains. Then she wrapped herself inside one. She was hiding from the other kangaroos! She felt safe with the Richardses. They were her family.

The president of the Royal Society for the Prevention of Cruelty to Animals (RSPCA) heard about Lulu's courage. The RSPCA gives a special award for bravery to animals that have helped humans in an unusual way. The RSPCA's president said he hoped someone would nominate Lulu for the award. And someone did. Len never knew who it was.

People at the RSPCA met. They talked
it over. They decided that Lulu deserved
the national bravery
award. It was the ninth
time the award had been
given. But it was the
first time it had been
awarded to a native
Australian animal.

Len and Lynn went
to Melbourne to receive the medal. They
didn't take Lulu. It would be pretty hard to
squeeze those big feet into a car. When
they got home, Len presented the award to
Lulu. It was an honor, and she had earned
it. Lulu had saved Len's life. The little
kangaroo that Luke had rescued had
grown up to rescue Len!

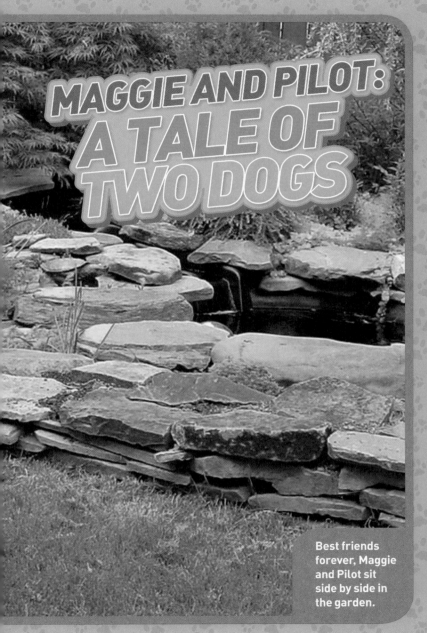

MAGGIE AND PILOT: A TALE OF TWO DOGS

Best friends forever, Maggie and Pilot sit side by side in the garden.

As a puppy, Maggie rarely stayed still. But she did for this picture!

Chapter 1

PLAY BALL

On a warm spring day, in Arlington, Virginia, U.S.A., Fred Edwards flopped onto the grass. He held a squirming puppy on his chest. She licked his face and scampered down. The eight-week-old puppy romped in the grass. Then she spied some yellow tulip blossoms. Chomp!

The puppy was named Magellan (sounds like muh-JELL-un), after a famous explorer. But her nickname was Maggie. Earlier that day, Fred and his wife, Cathy Jamieson, had fetched Maggie from a breeder. The breeder was a friend of Fred's. He had picked out this puppy just for them.

"The breeder told us she was a plump puppy who lounged on her back a lot. That meant she was confident and relaxed," Cathy said.

The puppy was happy and friendly, just like the breeder had promised. Cathy and Fred soon fell completely in love with Maggie. And after a few weeks, Fred said, "Maggie needs a sister."

Cathy had been thinking the same thing. So she called the breeder.

"Maggie's father is the father of another

litter of puppies," Cathy told Fred. "They were just born. What do you think?"

Fred didn't have to think. He and Cathy jumped in the car. Just one month after getting Maggie, they picked up a second puppy—Maggie's half sister.

This puppy was black. Fred and Cathy named her Pilot, like someone who steers a plane or a boat. That would turn out to be a very good name!

Maggie and Pilot were both Labrador retrievers (sounds like LAB-ruh-door ree-TREE-vurz). But they were as different as their colors. Maggie was outgoing and friendly. Pilot liked to just watch. She was on the shy side, except where Maggie was concerned. Pilot immediately formed a special friendship with her. She followed

Maggie everywhere. Cathy learned that it's common for two dogs close in age like Maggie and Pilot to have a strong bond.

Retrievers are hunting dogs. They fetch birds for hunters. And like most retrievers, Maggie loved to fetch. She would run after her tennis ball and bring it back—over and over. Eventually Fred got tired of throwing it!

But Pilot never bothered chasing balls. "She seemed to think it was silly," said Cathy. Pilot had a different interest. Pilot loved socks. She loved underwear, too. If Fred was changing, Pilot would sneak up behind him. She would flatten herself on the floor and wait quietly. Then, when Fred dropped his socks or underpants on the floor—pounce! She would snatch them and run away!

As the puppies grew, they started teething. That meant they were losing their baby teeth and getting adult teeth. And it meant they liked to chew.

When Fred asked, "Where are the puppies?" Cathy usually had a pretty good idea. She looked under the dining room table. Sure enough, they were underneath it. And they were gnawing on their favorite thing—chair legs. Sometimes Cathy even found the puppy teeth they lost.

Whenever Cathy and Fred went out, they put the puppies in crates. Cathy didn't want Maggie and Pilot to chew things up. One day, Cathy and Fred decided to test the puppies. They didn't lock them in their crates. Uh oh! When they came back, they found strings and stuffing and fabric bits all over. The pups had shredded the arm of the sofa. Maybe they weren't quite ready for freedom yet!

The puppies chased each other all over the house. They tumbled and wrestled. But they always stayed on the first floor of the house. They were afraid of the stairs!

"It's time they learned how to climb the stairs," Fred said one day. "Here, Maggie," he called. He held out a treat. Cautiously, Maggie hopped up one step and stopped.

"Come on, Pilot," Cathy called, holding out another nibble. Pilot tried a step, too. Step by step, the pups crawled up. After each step, they gobbled up a treat. It wasn't long before they could leap up and down the stairs. Soon Cathy and Fred wondered why they had taught them. Now the puppies were racing everywhere!

In time, Pilot and Maggie grew into healthy adult dogs. They were trained now and didn't need Cathy's attention all the time. One day Cathy heard about an organization that trained guide dogs for people who were blind. They were looking for people to help train puppies. She volunteered.

Cathy and Fred began taking puppies. They would keep them a few weeks. They taught them to "sit" and "stay." Meanwhile, Maggie and Pilot showed them how to behave with other dogs.

Did You Know?

Labradors are the breed of dog most often used in guide dog programs around the world.

Maggie loved to play with the puppies. But she could only put up with them for so long. When she was tired, she walked away. Pilot played with them for hours. She even let the pups nibble on her ears and her belly. If they nipped too hard, she growled softly. This helped train the puppies, too.

When Maggie was around four years old, Cathy noticed a change in her behavior. "She had a little trouble fetching her ball," said Cathy. "She seemed to lose sight of it." Fred and Cathy were worried. Maggie was usually a master fetcher. Was she having trouble seeing?

They took Maggie to the veterinarian (sounds like vet-er-ih-NARE-ee-en). The vet had sad news for them. Poor Maggie had a terrible eye disease. She was going blind.

Guide Dogs

Several organizations breed and train dogs to guide people who are blind. It takes a special dog to be a guide dog. It must be confident. It can't be easily distracted. Dogs in guide dog programs are taught special commands. They learn to ignore other people and dogs when they are working. Finally, guide dogs are taught to ignore what their owner tells them sometimes. That way a guide dog can protect its owner from stepping into a street if a car is coming!

Sniff, sniff! Maggie uses her nose to check out a sweet-smelling gingerbread house.

LOOK OUT!

Maggie's vet sent her to a special eye doctor for dogs. This doctor explained that Maggie would probably lose her eyesight completely in about six months. Cathy and Fred were heartbroken.

What could they do to help their beloved dog? Cathy wondered. They read books about living with blind dogs. They learned that there were some things they could do to make life easier for Maggie.

First, they should make sure they didn't leave things on the floor. That way she wouldn't trip. They also learned that they should not move the furniture around. And when they took Maggie to a new place, they should always walk her around the perimeter (sounds like puh-RIM-uh-tur), or outside edge, of the place.

Cathy and Fred also started giving Maggie word and sound clues. They told her if a curb was nearby. And they tapped or patted surfaces, like the sofa, if they wanted her to jump up.

Experts say that blind dogs usually slow down a bit. They are more cautious (sounds like CAW-shus), and they like to be on a leash. Dogs that lose their eyesight often don't want to run anymore.

But the experts didn't know Maggie. This brave dog didn't slow down one bit.

Then, one day Cathy and Fred got some more bad news. They learned that Maggie had another eye disease—glaucoma (sounds like glah-KO-muh). This disease put pressure on her eyes. There was no cure. Maggie would have to have her eyes removed.

After her surgery, Maggie was more energetic than ever. Cathy and Fred were puzzled. Then they realized that the disease had probably given Maggie headaches. Now she felt better!

Maggie showed Cathy and Fred that she could use her other senses. Dogs have very sensitive noses. They can smell

100,000 times better than humans can! So if a dog loses its sight, it can use its sense of smell to make up for it. Dogs can also use their sense of touch. They can find their way by feeling things with their whiskers.

One day Cathy took Maggie to a store. Maggie started digging under an appliance.

"Maggie, stop," said Cathy. But Maggie paid no attention. Cathy went over to her and bent down. Sure enough, there was a tennis ball underneath!

During the holidays, Cathy always made a gingerbread house. She decorated it with frosting and yummy gumdrops. She made the fence out of pretzel pieces. Cathy put the gingerbread house on a table, like she always did. Pilot and Maggie knew not to touch it.

But Maggie sniffed the air. *Mmmmm.* Maybe she hoped the rules didn't apply now that she was blind. Or maybe the smell was too good. Maggie waited until she thought Cathy was not in the room.

Then Maggie tiptoed around the gingerbread house. Carefully, she removed all the pretzels and gobbled them up. But she didn't touch anything else!

Like most Labrador retrievers, Maggie and Pilot liked to swim. Sometimes, Cathy and Fred took them to an animal swimming center. The center had three pools. Two were long and narrow with ramps on both ends. The third was large and 12 feet (3.7 m) deep.

Did You Know?

When it swims, the Labrador retriever uses its strong paddle-like tail to steer.

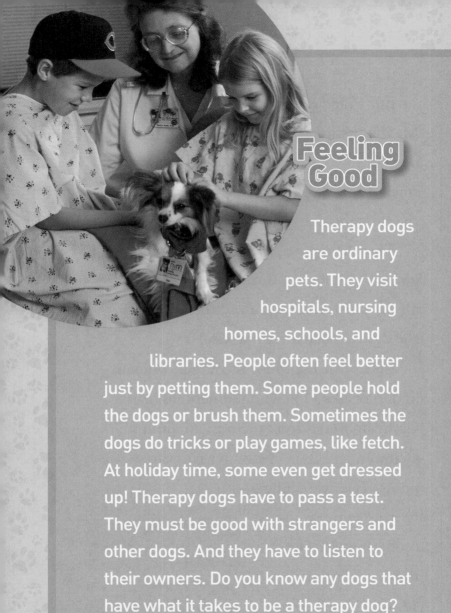

Feeling Good

Therapy dogs are ordinary pets. They visit hospitals, nursing homes, schools, and libraries. People often feel better just by petting them. Some people hold the dogs or brush them. Sometimes the dogs do tricks or play games, like fetch. At holiday time, some even get dressed up! Therapy dogs have to pass a test. They must be good with strangers and other dogs. And they have to listen to their owners. Do you know any dogs that have what it takes to be a therapy dog?

Cathy and Fred threw a tennis ball into one of the narrow pools. Splash! Maggie heard the ball slap the water. Then she dove in. She swam right to the ball!

But one day, Maggie decided that wasn't good enough. She heard the fun in the big pool. So she fetched her ball from the narrow pool. Then she ran to the large pool. Before Cathy could stop her, she jumped in! Other dog owners helped coax Maggie out. Cathy and Fred led her back to the narrow pool and threw her ball.

Moments later, Maggie was right back in the big pool. No eyes did not mean no fun!

Maggie was such a friendly dog that Cathy thought she would make a good therapy (sounds like THER-uh-pee) dog. Therapy dogs visit people in nursing homes and hospitals. Sick people are often cheered up by visits from friendly animals.

Maggie was happy to let people pet her. Sometimes she put her paw or head in their laps. "She seemed to know what to do for each person," said Cathy.

One time, Maggie did something amazing. Cathy took Maggie to visit a woman who was in bed. The woman had tubes attached to her for medicine.

Cathy tapped the bed so Maggie could put her paws up. But instead, Maggie leapt through the air. In an instant, she flew across the woman. Somehow, Maggie landed on the bed between the lady and

Did You Know?

Studies show that petting a dog can lower a person's blood pressure!

the wall. She hadn't pulled out any tubes. And best of all, she had made the lady so happy!

Cathy and Fred were glad that Maggie had adapted so well to her blindness. But now they started to notice some troubling changes in Pilot's behavior.

Maggie and Pilot did everything together—even take naps!

Chapter 3

EYES and EARS

Pilot had always been calm and gentle with the guide dog puppies. But now she had less patience with them. She growled at them more often. Then one day she even growled at a little girl who was passing by the house.

"That's not like Pilot," Cathy said. So Fred and Cathy visited an expert on dog behavior. They took the dogs with them. And they discovered something surprising.

Maggie had always been the leader in their house, the boss dog. But now that Maggie had lost her sight, Pilot was leading her around. Maybe Pilot had learned from the guide dog puppies in training. Perhaps it was just that she loved Maggie so much. Whatever the reason, Pilot was Maggie's guide dog!

But Fred and Cathy were still treating Maggie like the leader. And Pilot was getting upset. She wanted them to see that she was the boss now. The expert said that Pilot should be treated as the leader.

So Cathy and Fred made some changes. Now they fed Pilot first. They handed her treats first. They brushed her first. And they let her go outside ahead of Maggie.

The expert said that these were signs of respect for the top dog. Immediately, both Maggie and Pilot relaxed—except when they gave Pilot doggie ice cream first. Maggie stomped her feet at that!

Now Fred and Cathy started to see things they hadn't noticed before. Pilot walked very close to Maggie. Especially in crowds. She brushed Maggie's shoulder to show her the way. If there was an animal nearby, Pilot growled to alert Maggie.

Pilot even covered up for Maggie. One day, Fred and Cathy were out for a long time. When they opened the door, they stepped into a puddle. One of the dogs had had an accident in the house. Maggie greeted them as if nothing was wrong. But Pilot was hiding in the closet.

Fred and Cathy assumed Pilot had made the mess. But when they took the dogs outside, only Pilot went to the bathroom. Cathy realized that Maggie had had the accident. And Pilot took the blame for her!

Fred and Cathy spent a lot of time in Florida, U.S.A. To get there, they drove down. That way they could take "their girls" with them. In Florida, Fred and Cathy took the dogs to the beach. Both dogs ran into the water, like always. But now, Pilot swam right next to Maggie. She made sure she was touching her all the time.

Fred and Cathy owned a sailboat in Florida. Maggie and Pilot always went sailing with them. The two dogs had learned to jump across the water to get onto the boat.

Through a Dog's Eyes

Dogs' sight is different from humans'. They don't see colors as well, especially red. And they don't make out as many details as people do. But there are some things they see better than people. Dogs spot motion better. Breeds like shepherds, which herd sheep, notice even the smallest motions. These motions tell them that the herd is about to move. Dogs' eyes are farther apart than people's eyes. That way they can see things that are on the side better than humans can.

But now that Maggie couldn't see, Fred was afraid she might walk off the dock into the water. They tapped the deck. Maggie seemed to know that there was water nearby. So she jumped like she always did. But sometimes they had to dock the boat headfirst. That end was narrow, so if Maggie missed, she would fall in. Fred and Cathy made a harness for her. Then they swung Maggie out over the deck of the boat. She was never afraid!

When they were on the boat, Maggie knew to stay in the cockpit. That's the low area in the center of the boat. But she put her nose in the air to sniff the sea breeze. Pilot stayed nearby to make sure Maggie didn't fall overboard.

One day Cathy and Fred and "the girls" were at the beach in Key West, Florida. Fred was swimming far out. He had Pilot on a long leash with him. Cathy and Maggie were also in the water, closer to shore. A large pelican was swimming nearby. It kept getting closer.

Suddenly, the pelican swam right up to Maggie. It put its huge bill around her head. It tried to scoop Maggie up like a fish! Cathy screamed. But not as loudly as Pilot. Pilot made a screechy sound and swam toward the pelican. She scared the pelican away. Pilot saved Maggie from being badly hurt!

Did You Know?

Dogs have three eyelids. You can't usually see the third lid, but it protects their eyes and helps keep them moist.

When Maggie was 12 years old, she passed away peacefully. Fred and Cathy were sad. But they had Pilot to take care of. The first evening after Maggie died, Pilot was snoozing on the old basement sofa she had shared with Maggie. Fred and Cathy opened the kitchen cabinet to get her dinner. But Pilot didn't come upstairs. Usually the dogs came running when they heard the sound of food being put into bowls.

"Pilot! Dinnertime!" they called. She still didn't come.

Now they were worried. They thudded down the stairs. Pilot must have seen or felt their movement. She lifted her head and looked at them, surprised. Fred and Cathy looked at each other. Hadn't she heard them calling? By that evening, Cathy and Fred had figured out the truth. Pilot was completely deaf! Not only that, Maggie had been helping her to "hear."

Fred and Cathy didn't know how long ago Pilot had lost her hearing. But from that moment on, she stayed close to them so she could see them. Pilot was getting older, too. Cathy and Fred would need to help her get by in her silent world.

Pilot and Maggie were very brave dogs. They both had problems that made their lives challenging. But they were never afraid. More important, they were best friends. And like best friends, they helped each other. Pilot was Maggie's eyes. And Maggie was Pilot's ears. Together, they were each other's heroes.

Buttercup tries to steal a kiss from Lois Brady.

DASIEY, LULU, AND BUTTERCUP: THREE Little PIG HEROES

Jordan Jones and his pal Dasiey play together in the yard.

It was an ordinary fall day. Seven-year-old Jordan Jones was playing in his front yard in Las Vegas, Nevada, U.S.A., with his best friend, Dasiey (sounds like DAY-zee).

Suddenly, Jordan heard frantic barking, followed by a deep growl. And then—crack! Something broke. The next-door neighbor's dog had broken through the fence. And it was charging toward him!

Most dogs are friendly to humans. But sometimes they can be dangerous—like this dog. It was growling and snapping. Jordan was terrified. He froze.

Luckily, his friend Dasiey knew what to do. Dasiey wasn't a person. She was the family's 150-pound (68-kg) pet pig. Squeal! She jumped in front of the dog. The dog lunged at Dasiey.

Jordan's mother heard the commotion and ran outside. The dog had backed Dasiey into a corner. But Dasiey stood tall. So the dog clamped onto Dasiey's ear. Squeal! The dog shook Dasiey's head. Poor Dasiey was bleeding. But she still didn't give up!

The dog's owner tried to get the dog to let go of Dasiey. But it wouldn't. Jordan's mother screamed for Jordan's father. Somehow, he separated the dog and the pig.

Jordan was shaking. But he was fine. Unfortunately, Dasiey was hurt. Her ear was partly torn off. And her face was cut and bleeding. Jordan's mother called a vet.

The vet said that the wounds on Dasiey's face would heal by themselves. But he had to stitch up her ear. It healed too, but always drooped a little. It was a reminder of how brave she had been.

"Dasiey will always be our hero," said Jordan's mother.

How did this brave pig come into Jordan's life? The Jones family bought the black-and-white potbellied piglet as a pet for Jordan. They named her Dasiey. Potbellied pigs are originally from Vietnam (sounds like vee-et-NAHM). They are smaller than American farm pigs.

Like many potbellied pigs, Dasiey was confident and friendly. Potbellied pigs are protective of their herd. When they live in homes with people, they treat their human family like their herd. That's why she put herself in front of the dog when it attacked Jordan.

A year after Dasiey rescued Jordan, his family learned that they had to move away from Las Vegas. They couldn't take Dasiey with them. They were heartbroken.

Mrs. Jones called a pig rescue organization. Pig rescue groups find new homes for pigs when their families can't keep them. At first, no one offered to take Dasiey. Then a woman named Kim

Moneymaker said she would adopt the brave little pig. Her family already had two pigs.

Kim lived in Raymond, California, U.S.A., near Yosemite (sounds like yoh-SEH-muh-tee). She and Mrs. Jones agreed to meet halfway. Together they loaded Dasiey into Kim's van.

Mrs. Jones patted the pig. "Watch your trash," she told Kim. "She's a trash feeder!"

Jordan didn't offer any advice. He just gave Dasiey a big hug. Then he burst into tears. It's not easy to say goodbye to your best friend.

On the ride home, Dasiey fidgeted. Then she started breathing hard. Kim pulled off the highway. She and her sons, Mathew and Daniel, petted the stressed piggy.

"It will be OK," they said. "We're taking you to a new home."

Dasiey seemed to understand. She relaxed and rolled onto her side. As soon as they got home, Kim and the boys lifted Dasiey out of the car. Then she did the strangest thing.

"She kicked up her back legs, like a donkey," said Kim. "Then she was fine!"

Kim showed Dasiey her bed. It was in a giant doghouse right by their front door. But it was outside. Dasiey wanted to be inside. With the tip of her nose, she opened the screen door. Then she pushed her snout against the front door. Bam! Bam!

Kim felt sorry for the sweet pig. She opened the door.

Dogs and Hogs

Dogs and hogs aren't natural friends.
They usually stay away from each other.
And sometimes, a dog will view a pig as,
well, food. But occasionally, a dog and a
pig find that they have a special bond.
Runty, a young pig in northern England,
kept escaping from her pen. She dug
under the wire fence. And she went to
the same place every time—the dog
kennel! She curled up with one of her
owner's dogs—a terrier named Alfie.
They had become best friends.

Dasiey strolled into the house, flopped down, and fell asleep. The next morning, Kim found Dasiey underneath the sofa cushions. "I guess you're going to be an inside pig," she said.

Now it was time for Dasiey to meet the family's other two pigs. *Would she get along?* Kim didn't need to worry. Dasiey was sweet and easygoing. She fit right in.

Kim had a large, fenced-in ranch. That made it easy to take in more rescue pigs. One of them had piglets. The new additions slept outside in a pig house Kim built for them. But everyone ate together. They bumped and shoved each other to get at the food bowls—like kids on a bumper car ride!

A few years after getting Dasiey, Kim

adopted a rescue pig named Bogart. He
was shy and stayed by himself. Perhaps
he missed his old family.

Dasiey seemed to know Bogart needed
a friend. She stayed with him every day.
But at night, she still slept inside. Then,
one night, Dasiey banged on the door to go
out. *What's she up to?* Kim wondered.
Kim watched Dasiey waddle over to where
Bogart was dozing in the pig house. She
climbed in and snuggled under the straw
with him. From then on, Bogart was a
relaxed and happy pig, too.

Dasiey still lives with Kim and sleeps
with Bogart. Early on, she proved herself
to be a brave pig by rescuing Jordan. Later,
by helping Bogart, Dasiey showed she was
as bighearted as she was brave!

Lulu the pig sniffs her way through the grass. Maybe she's looking for something good to eat!

LOYAL
LULU

Dasiey is not the only pig that rescued her owner. Six years earlier, another potbellied pig saved her owner's life, too. It all began when Jack Altsman of Beaver Falls, Pennsylvania, U.S.A., gave his daughter a piglet. His wife, JoAnne, thought it was a mistake. Their daughter worked long hours. How could she take care of a pet pig?

Sure enough, not long after she got the pig, JoAnne's daughter needed a favor. Could JoAnne babysit the four-pound (1.8-kg) piglet? JoAnne's daughter told her that pigs were smart and affectionate. And besides, she only needed help for a week.

JoAnne took the black piglet from her daughter. Her daughter had named her Lulu. She peered into Lulu's eyes. Maybe she *was* kind of cute. JoAnne agreed to watch the pig—but only for a week!

Jack and JoAnne weren't happy about having Lulu join them. Neither was Bear, their American Eskimo dog. But two months later, Lulu was still living in JoAnne and Jack's home.

Lulu slept in JoAnne's living room.

Like most pigs, she was clean. She didn't make a mess. She was also easy to train. Best of all, Lulu was very friendly.

JoAnne came to love the pig. And Lulu loved JoAnne. It probably helped that JoAnne fed her jelly doughnuts, Lulu's favorite food in the world!

Thanks to those jelly doughnuts, Lulu grew and grew. Now poor Bear was tiny next to Lulu. A full-grown standard American Eskimo dog weighs no more than 35 pounds (16 kg). Lulu had gone from 4 pounds (1.8 kg) to 150 pounds (68 kg). That's average for an adult potbellied pig.

Did You Know?

Pigs have a good sense of direction. They have been known to find their way home over great distances.

Hog History

Scientists think that pigs, also known as hogs and swine, have existed on Earth for millions of years. Some kinds of wild pigs are called boars. Male hogs are also called boars. Females are called sows. And baby hogs are called piglets. Pigs will eat just about anything they can get their snouts on. They gobble up roots, grasses, fruits, nuts, mushrooms, worms, and even snakes. In fact, pigs can find food almost anywhere. That's probably why they have been around for so long!

Sometimes JoAnne's daughter asked for her pig back. But JoAnne was too attached to that little porker. And Lulu squealed whenever someone took her from JoAnne. Lulu was JoAnne's pig. And one day, JoAnne would be very glad that she was!

Lulu and JoAnne were always together. They ran errands together. They sat in the sun. Lulu sat in JoAnne's lap to watch television. Sometimes Lulu got hungry. She'd tiptoe up to the refrigerator and open the door with her snout. Then she would sneak a snack!

One fall weekend, JoAnne and Jack drove to a favorite fishing spot on Lake Erie. They took their trailer with them. Bear and Lulu went along.

Jack got up early the next morning.

He took his fishing pole and went off. JoAnne, Bear, and Lulu stayed in the trailer. JoAnne poured herself a cup of coffee. She opened a book. Suddenly, JoAnne felt a terrible tightness in her chest. She knew what the feeling meant—a heart attack.

JoAnne fell to the floor. She tried to get up. But she couldn't. She threw an alarm clock at the nearest window and broke it. She cried out, hoping someone would hear her.

Bear barked and barked. Lulu waddled over to JoAnne. She nudged her. But JoAnne couldn't move. Lulu looked down at her and cried big pig tears. Then she sprang into action.

Lulu stuck her nose in the dog door in the trailer. She tried to squeeze through.

But all those jelly doughnuts had caught up with her. She got stuck halfway.

Lulu didn't give up. She grunted and snorted. Finally, she heaved herself through the door. Poor Lulu scraped her tender belly.

She pushed through a fence and ran to the nearest street to get help. She waited by the side of the road. When Lulu saw a car, she lumbered out in front of the car and sat down. Right in the middle of the lane. But the car drove around her. She went back to check on JoAnne. Then she tried again. No one stopped.

Finally, she rolled on her back. She stuck her hooves up in the air. She stared at the next driver to come along.

The young man stopped. He wondered what was wrong with her.

Lulu stood up. *Wee! Wee!* She squealed and started walking toward the trailer. The man felt a little silly. But something made him follow her.

When they got to the trailer, he knocked on the door. "I think your pig's in distress!"

JoAnne called back, "I'm in distress!" She told him she was having a heart attack.

The man called 9-1-1. An ambulance arrived. JoAnne was loaded in. Lulu tried to climb in, too! But there were no pigs allowed.

The ambulance whisked JoAnne to a hospital. The doctors said that if JoAnne had arrived 15 minutes later, she would have died.

When JoAnne finally came home from the hospital, Lulu broke through the screen door and ran up to her. She was so happy to see her beloved owner again.

Reporters wrote stories about Lulu's rescue. Lulu appeared on TV. One TV show offered a reward to the man who stopped for Lulu that day. But his identity is still a mystery. The American Society for the Prevention of Cruelty to Animals (ASPCA) gave Lulu a gold medal. The ceremony was held at a hotel in New York, U.S.A. A famous movie star brought his pet pig, Ralph, to help out!

Fame didn't change Lulu. She didn't mind the attention. But all she really wanted was to be by JoAnne's side. And to get an extra jelly doughnut!

Everyone loves to pet Buttercup's wiry hair and stroke her velvety ears.

Chapter 3

SWEET Little Buttercup

Have you ever noticed how people love to talk to animals? They talk to dogs, cats, and even hamsters and fish. Lois Brady noticed this one day when she and her students were on a field trip. They were hot and tired. Then a woman with a large dog walked by.

Immediately teachers and students jumped up and ran over

to the dog. They petted it and talked to it. Some of the students talked about the dog later. That was unusual for Lois's students. And it gave her an idea.

Lois is a speech therapist (sounds like THER-uh-pist). She works in a special school in California. It is a school for children with autism (sounds like AW-tiz-um). Autism is a brain disorder. It can make talking and other communication hard. That's why it surprised Lois when her students talked about the dog on the field trip.

Lois knew that many children with autism love animals. *Maybe having an animal in the classroom would help some of them talk,* she thought. But what kind of animal?

Riding and petting horses can calm some people. But horses are too big for the classroom. Most dogs are friendly to people. But they bark. And children with autism are extra sensitive to noises. She thought about rabbits. They are soft, but too fragile. And then a thought came to her. *What about a pig?*

Pigs are calm and quiet. They're sturdy. And they're interesting to touch. Their hair is wiry, their snouts are rubbery. Behind their ears is a soft velvet spot. And, unlike what many people think, pigs are clean and don't smell.

Did You Know?

China has more domestic, or tame, pigs than any other country in the world. The United States has the second largest number of pigs.

Pig Chatter

Pigs are social animals. That means they live together in groups and communicate with each other. Pigs make over 20 different oinks, grunts, and squeals. A short grunt means the pig is excited. A long grunt is how one pig calls to another. A pig that is injured or upset will squeal. A boss pig will threaten another pig with a barking noise. And a mother pig will sing to her piglets when she is feeding them. And, of course, pigs make a lot of noise when they are hungry!

Lois set out to find the perfect pig. Soon, she found a breeder in Texas.

"We have a four-week-old potbellied piglet," they told her.

"I'll take him," Lois said.

Lois and her family went to the airport in nearby San Francisco, California. They found the piglet waiting for them in a small crate. Lois opened the crate. A tiny black piglet about the size of a guinea (sounds like GIH-nee) pig stepped out. Lois picked him up.

"Hello, my little cutie," she said. The pig tucked his little snout in between her elbow and her body. And he stayed like that the entire ride home.

At home, Lois settled the little pig in the kitchen area. He would stay there during the day. Her children played with him all day long. Like most pigs, he loved to have his belly rubbed. Lois discovered that if she scratched his back, he would immediately drop down and roll over for a belly rub!

"Now, what shall we name you?" she asked the pig. Lois wanted to give him a name with a lot of different sounds in it. That way her students could practice saying something that might be hard for them. She picked the name "Buttercup."

Buttercups are sweet, cheerful flowers. Buttercup the pig was sweet and cheerful, too—except when food was around. Then the little hog acted like, well, a hog. He loved to eat—especially watermelon. He even ate the seeds!

When Buttercup was two months old, Lois took him to visit her son's second grade class. As she hoped, Buttercup was calm and friendly.

Lois decided Buttercup was ready to meet her students. The pig was still small. Lois tucked him inside her coat and took him to her class.

"I want you to sit in a large circle," she told her students. She reached inside her coat. She pulled out

the piggy. Then she set Buttercup on the floor. That sweet little porker tiptoed up to each student. He climbed into their laps. Then, just like he did with Lois, he snuggled his snout into their elbows.

Everyone wanted a turn with him. Some were willing to try to make a sound or to try to say "hi" just to be allowed to pet him.

Not long afterward, Lois got a new student. The boy had been teased and bullied in his old school. Now he was frightened. He hid under a desk. He refused to talk. He wouldn't even look at the other kids. But he liked animals.

Could Buttercup help him? Lois wondered. The next day, she brought Buttercup to school. She kept the other students out of the classroom at first. The boy was under the desk, as usual. But the moment he saw Buttercup, everything changed. He scrambled out to pet Buttercup. He talked to him. His words were hard to understand. But he seemed to be asking the pig questions.

Then Lois let the other students into the room. The boy didn't crawl back under his desk. Instead, he took Buttercup's leash and led him outside to go potty. Then the boy did something amazing. He called to the other students. He wanted them to come over to meet the pig.

From that moment on, this boy left his silent world. The next couple of mornings, he started out by sitting under a desk. But after only a little while, he came out. He tried to talk to two other students about the pig. They soon became friends with him.

Now this boy shakes people's hands. He asks them their names. He has made huge improvements, all thanks to Buttercup!

At home, Buttercup is the family pet. He cuddles with the kids when they watch TV. He wags his curly pig tail when he hears Lois's voice. And he crawls under any dirty clothes he finds on the floor!

These days, Buttercup visits Lois's school regularly. Students get excited as soon as they see him in the parking lot. Over the years, he has made a difference in many children's lives. In his quiet way, Buttercup is a hero to Lois's students!

THE END

DON'T MISS!

NATIONAL GEOGRAPHIC KiDS **CHAPTERS**

HORSE ESCAPE ARTIST!

And More True Stories of **Animals Behaving Badly**

By Ashlee Brown Blewett

Turn the page for a sneak preview . . .

Milkshake looks ready to party in her purple cowboy hat, but first she stops to pose for the camera. Say "cheese"!

MILKSHAKE: THE CHARGING COW

Milkshake is ready to be led on a walk around the Grace Foundation.

Chapter 1

No Ordinary COW

The sound of heavy hooves hitting cement echoed through a large ranch in El Dorado Hills, California, U.S.A. CLOP. CLOP. CLOP. Milkshake the cow moseyed up the sidewalk. She stopped outside an open door and looked up. A wooden sign read "Cowgirls." Milkshake entered.

Outside the sun shone bright. But inside the room was dim.

It took the cow's eyes time to adjust. When they did, Milkshake found herself standing in front of a sink. She was in the ranch's bathroom. She glanced up at a large mirror on the wall. Her eyes widened. *Humph!* She blew a puff of air through her nose.

Staring back at Milkshake was another cow. It looked just like her. *Yikes!*

Milkshake panicked. She shuffled her burly body backward. Clatter, bang, boom! A trash can crashed to the floor. Dust flew. Milkshake bolted out the bathroom door like a high-speed bullet train.

It was the first time the cow had seen her reflection. But what in the world was a cow doing in a bathroom?

Milkshake is no ordinary cow. And the ranch where Milkshake lives is no ordinary ranch. It's home to the Grace Foundation. Grace is a group that rescues animals whose owners don't take care of them.

Grace's goal is to make each animal better. They bring in veterinarians (sounds like vet-er-ih-NARE-ee-ens) to treat the animals that are hurt or sick.

There are many horses at Grace, along with some cows, sheep, llamas, chickens, and other animals. As soon as an animal is healthy, Grace usually looks for a loving family to adopt it. But a few of the rescued animals get to stay at Grace for good.

The animals that stay have important jobs. They are called animal educators. They help teach children who visit the ranch about farm animals. Today Milkshake is one of the animal educators. But her first few months at Grace were rocky.

Milkshake arrived at the ranch in 2008. She was small and shy. She was about two years old. Her previous owner had kept her locked in a filthy pen. The pen was so small it stunted, or slowed down, Milkshake's growth.

Milkshake is a Hereford (sounds like HER-furd) cow. Herefords are a large breed of cattle. A two-year-old normally weighs about 1,000 pounds (450 kg). But Milkshake weighed only half that!

Besides locking Milkshake in a tiny pen, Milkshake's owner didn't talk to her. She didn't pet her. And she separated Milkshake from other animals.

Cow Chow

Most cows eat grass. But grass is not an easy food to digest. This makes eating an all-day task. First, good bacteria in the cow's stomach help break down the grass. Then the cow spits up partly digested food called cud. It chews the cud for about eight hours. Then—GULP!—the cow swallows the cud. It travels back through the cow's four-part stomach where more bacteria help the cow digest the food for good.

INDEX

Boldface indicates illustrations.

MORE INFORMATION

To find more information about the animal species featured in this book, check out these books and websites:

How to Speak Dog, by Aline Alexander Newman and Gary Weitzman, National Geographic, 2013.

National Geographic Kids Everything Dogs, by Becky Baines, National Geographic, 2012.

Animal-Assisted Speech Therapy
www.animalassistedspeechtherapy.com

Guiding Eyes for the Blind
guidingeyes.org

National Geographic Kids "Kangaroo"
kids.nationalgeographic.com/animals/kangaroo.html

National Geographic Kids "Pig"
kids.nationalgeographic.com/animals/pig.html

The Story of Lulu the Kangaroo
youtube.com/watch?v=yVz0dH7gGtQ

To Ellen Braaf and the members of
the SCBWI Mid-Atlantic Region, my writing family.

CREDITS

ACKNOWLEDGMENTS

My special thanks to the following people who helped in this project:

My amazingly talented editors, Marfé Ferguson Delano and Shelby
Alinsky, who made this book so much better than it was.

Len Richards, human companion of Lulu the kangaroo, for taking time
to talk to me all the way from Australia.

Cathy Jamieson and Fred Edwards, owners of Maggie and Pilot, for
their generosity and for being such incredible dog lovers.

Dr. Gary Schrader and the staff at Suburban Animal Hospital, for
sharing Maggie and Pilot's story.

Minnie Gallman, for vetting the information about guide dogs.

Kim Moneymaker, current caretaker of the brave pig, Dasiey, for
all her help.

Lois Brady, for her kind assistance and her phenomenal work
with Buttercup.

And, as always, my supportive family.